BUYERS ARE LIARS
& SELLERS ARE TOO!

*A Lighthearted Look at the Truth About
Buying and Selling Your Home*

RICHARD COURTNEY

Edited by Paine Wolfe

Design, typography, and production by JM Productions, Inc., Brentwood, Tennessee

ISBN: 0-9635026-0-3

Library of Congress Catalog Card Number: 92-74959

Eggman Publishing
2908 Poston Avenue, Suite 201
Nashville, Tennessee 37203

This book is

Presented to:

_____

_____

_____

By:

With great confidence that you will never, ever become a
liar, an ogre, an ET, or a Greedledee or a Greedledum

Disclaimer

If you're going to dabble in the real estate world, you need to get used to this word. Here, however, it has nothing to do with real estate...only this book. The characters to which I refer are composites of people with whom I have dealt, as well as the clients and customers of my esteemed colleagues.

About the Author

Oh, we're all just crazy about him.

Dedication

To all the people who loved all the houses

But not enough to pay that much for it. ("Show us something else.")

And to all the people who wanted to sell their houses

But not enough to take that little for it. ("We're not going to *give* it away.")

And with extreme gratitude to all of those in between. ("We'll take it.")

Contents

Introduction

A house is a place in which people reside, hence a residence — or more comfortably speaking, a home.

A house is not a home, however, until the successful completion of a series of events. The house is listed for sale, it is shown, a contract is negotiated, a loan is applied for and approved, the sale and the loan are closed, and possession is given. It all seems easy enough. Why, then, is it so terribly complicated? The answer is very simple:

Buyers are liars and sellers are too.

They are not born liars, and most do not want to be. After reading this book, maybe both buyers and sellers will become more truthful. Buyers will know more about sellers, and sellers will empathize more with buyers.

And, if we're lucky, the agents of the sellers and the agents of the buyers also will better understand each other. This will lead to total peace in the real-estatic world in which we exist. The achievement of this harmonious state is the purpose of this book. Your efforts and contributions toward this end are greatly appreciated.

Chapter 1

The REALTOR

No Place for Barney Fife

Barney Fife, self-regarded hero of Mayberry, North Carolina, is a man of great ambition, a man whose keen entrepreneurial mind is as finely tuned as his agile physique. Barney once saw a great opportunity to make quick bucks in the field of real estate. He saw real estate sales as one, big domino game.

Barney's plan was intricate and could have worked. He would sell Mr. and Mrs. Clark the home of Mr. and Mrs. Morton, who in turn would buy the house owned by the Simmses, who would then purchase the home of Sheriff Taylor, who would buy the residence of Mr. Williams. Easy enough. The deal soured, however, when young Opie Taylor disclosed some of his home's deficiencies to Mr. and Mrs. Simms.

At first Andy and Barney tried to discount Opie's observations and downplayed the home's leaks and cracks almost to the point of denial. Yes, it's sad to say. But when placed in the role of a seller, even Andy Taylor, Mayberry's finest, was tempted to lie. Andy later recanted his denial and coverup, and was pardoned by Gerald Ford (I think). As for Barney, in his zeal to close the deal, he had breached his fiduciary duty to the Simmses and proved that he was certainly not a REALTOR.

REALTORS are different from real estate agents. They

1

have passed a course that teaches them not to lie. They pay a bunch of money to their local board of REALTORS and the National Board of REALTORS. These memberships allow them to receive several trade magazines featuring articles concerning all the scuttlebutt going on in the real estate world.

This rare breed of masochists also attends luncheons and the like, and they devote all of their days (evenings and weekends included) to the pursuit of happiness and homefulness for their clients. Their cars are often the site of infantile vomitus explosions and other accidents.

Their home phone rings all hours of the day and night with callers wanting to know everything, such as why their interest rate is one figure and the APR (annual percentage rate) is another on a home that closed twelve years ago. Or they may even want to know the distance between the commode and the shower on their listing on Plum Street.

Or, "Why isn't the loan survey deductible? What if I deduct it? Would you write me a letter saying I can deduct it? By the way, a neighbor's tree fell in my yard and he won't remove it. Will the lawyer who closed the loan handle this for me? Free? He was a friend of yours, wasn't he?"

Some people feel REALTORS are overpaid. If your REALTOR doesn't earn every penny of his commission, it's your fault. Ask your REALTOR questions, and more importantly, listen to his answers. Your REALTOR knows what the houses sell for in the area in which you want to buy. You must tell him where you want to buy. Make him show you comparable closed sales in the area. Ask him which lenders provide good service and good rates. One without the other is useless.

Let your REALTOR assist you in having a competent real estate attorney close your loan. Atticus Finch was a great killer of rabid dogs and protector of human and civil rights, and he led a wonderful crusade to save the mockingbird from extinction; however, he might not be able to prepare a deed of trust or a warranty deed or provide clear title to a property. By the same token, the fellow who lost six hundred straight lawsuits to Perry Mason might have been a wonderful real estate attorney. Unfortunately, there is not much glamour in it.

Your REALTOR will also know inspectors who know how to inspect a home rather than critique it. Of course, you may *want* your home critiqued, in which case that can be done too.

If you are listing your property, REALTORS have the resources to price it, the network to market it, the expertise to aid in the negotiations, and the persistence to make it happen. And they don't make a penny until the deal is done. Make them work for it. They asked for it when they got into this crazy, at times entertaining, business.

Now, to be fair, all REALTORS are not equally good. Some are mediocre...yes, perhaps even horrible. But most are conscientious, professional, and effective. Find one. Your selection can mean a real treat or your worst nightmare. You are going to eat with them, ride in their cars, have them in your home, and meet in their offices. Check them out, and when you find one you like, roll with him or her. Your loyalty will motivate your REALTOR to do a better job for you.

If you attend open houses, tell the attending agent that you have an agent and name the agent. The open house agent won't hate you and throw you out. As a matter of fact, he will appreciate it because he will know that he can call one of his colleagues and learn all about you without having to be nice to you.

The following chapters will better explain each aspect of the home-buying process from the perspective of:

- Seller
- Seller's Agent
- Buyer
- Buyer's Agent

Along with some helpful hints, the discussions are flavored

with some colorful examples of how you might have performed in your role as buyer or seller had you not gained the tremendous wisdom provided in this book. You will also better understand why one, skinny deputy in North Carolina nipped his real estate career in the bud.

Chapter 2

The Listing

The Greatest Showing on Earth

P.T. Barnum has been credited with saying that there is a sucker born every minute. Most homeowners take great stock in that adage, and most real estate agents must have a big "S" magically tattooed on their foreheads in such a fashion that the letter only appears at listing presentations. For it is at that time that caution, comparable sales information, current market conditions, and reason are thrown to the wind.

These potential sellers have decided for some reason to move, even though they are leaving the best house ever designed and constructed. The Taj Mahal pales in comparison with this home, chocked so full of amenities and representing a value so great that to sacrifice this home at true market value (plus about twenty-five percent) will assure the sellers of automatic sainthood.

Many sellers seem to believe this themselves. That's when it really gets scary. I once had a client who had a house with over 2,600 square feet and had no central air conditioning. He tried to explain to me how to arrange the windows, doors, and furniture so as to provide a draft that was more beneficial to the human body than air generated by that horrid ozone killer, freon.

Then, nobly combining generosity with ecology, he refused to penalize any would-be buyers by charging extra for his priceless cooling system. Yes, he would condescend to list his house for an amount equal to a similar house that had central heat and air. And, believe it or not, he was a reasonable man in real life.

At this point, we introduce the aforementioned format that will prevail in the chapters ahead.

SELLER

These people (or individual) have decided to leave their paradisical palace and have enlisted the aid of a real estate agent to help in their attempt to sell this property. Somehow they agreed to the list price and will most likely refuse, for at least six weeks, any offer that is not close to that price.

The sellers will continue to think their home is the greatest deal in town until either: 1) Ten or fifteen people have shown it with no offers resulting, or 2) No one has shown it. At that point, the sellers begin to taste realty reality, although some might instead blame their agents rather than accept responsibility for overpricing, market conditions, or the street appeal of their homes.

Hints to Seller:

- Make sure your house is clean every day. The one day you don't have it tidy, a transferee with a cleanliness fetish who has to buy a house that day will want to see it.

- Your cute, little, pet looks like King Kongzilla to some people, makes the allergics cry like babies, or conjures sad memories of a pet murdered by an evil stepfather. Take your pet away or have it comfortably penned if you are unable to remove it. Animal lovers revolt at mistreatment.

6

- Repair the little things that need it. Prior to the do-it-yourself home improvement craze, most people could not have told you whether a cracked door facing cost $5 or $500. If you lack the manual dexterity or expertise to repair the problem, please hire someone who does. I beg of thee. It's for your own good. Legend has it that someone once drywalled an entire room and was unaware that tape was needed at the joints.

- Make your house easy to show. And on short notice. If your agent calls for a spur-of-the-moment showing by another agent, don't yell at her. She is only trying to sell your home. Cooperate. Be gentle. Agents' egos are oh-so fragile.

- If your agent or the buyer's agent can't be present for a showing, never try to show your home by yourself. You are not trained in this area and even if you mean well, you'll blow it. So leave!

Case in point: Prospective buyers, a young couple, once asked a seller if there were children in the neighborhood. The seller, noting the youthfulness of the prospective buyers decided they would like children. "Oh yes, they're all over the place." That killed the deal. The prospective buyers hated children. No kidding. As it turned out, the area didn't have any more or any fewer children than other areas that the prospective buyers were considering.

SELLER'S AGENT

The seller's agent has made a listing presentation in order to gain the listing. This presentation usually includes a Comparative Market Analysis (CMA), which details the most recent sales in the area, the homes that are currently listed, and any sales that are pending. This report is actually more valuable than an appraisal, which would cost several hundred dollars.

Appraisals generally compare only three sold properties.

Usually the appraiser has never seen the interior of the comparable sales. On the other hand, if the seller's agent is active in the area, chances are good that she has shown (or even sold) most of the homes in the CMA. The agent will then price the new listing accordingly, if the seller will listen.

IMPORTANT: Note the "Days on Market" category of the CMA, which your real estate agent will know, but which an appraisal will not indicate. A house comparable to yours may have sold for a great price, but it might have taken seven years of being on the market.

Hints to Seller's Agent:

- Keep in touch with your seller.

- Try to follow up on showings and report back, but explain in advance that it may not always be possible to do so.

- If you agree to list the property at a price that is too high, remind the seller in writing that you feel it is too high. Sellers have a tendency to forget and then blame the listing agent when their home doesn't sell.

- Remember the property is your listing, but more importantly, it is the seller's home. Respect that.

BUYER'S AGENT

The buyer's agent has many ways of monitoring new listings in order to arrange for the Greatest Showing on Earth. These include driving through his areas and noting new signs, listening to word of mouth (or networking, if you will), and monitoring listings electronically through the Multiple Listing Service (MLS). The MLS is an invaluable information source of which all members are able to input and retrieve data for every property that is currently on the market or that has closed within the last year.

This MLS information is much more timely than any information that might be retrieved from the office of the Register of Deeds because the member users of the MLS enter the sales data immediately following the closing, whereas it could take the closing attorney a week or two to record the transfer. (We'll discuss this more in the "For Sale by Ogre" chapter.)

The buyer's agents communicate with seller's agents in establishing their great showings. They try to give the listing agent as much notice as possible prior to showing a property. However, it is not uncommon to stumble across a property while in the midst of showing other properties. Perhaps it is a new listing or looks better in person than it does electronically. During these times, the buyer's agents may call the seller's agent and ask to show the property on fifteen to thirty minutes notice. It is important to comply with these wishes because they probably will not return.

Hints to Buyer's Agent:

- Please make every effort to contact the listing (seller's) agent in order that they can report news and activity to the seller.

- Tell the truth (I know it hurts). If the property is overpriced, tell the seller's agent. The agent wants to know or, more probably, needs an excuse to tell the owner (seller) the perception of an unbiased person.

Hint About Buyer's Agent:

- He is not trying to "sell" the listing. He is guiding prospects through potential homes. If his buyer chooses another home, so be it. It is the buyer's choice. Don't expect your agent to try to sell the buyer's agent.

BUYER

He, she, or they are being shown properties that the agent

9

feels they would be interested in. The seller (property owner) needs to realize that these buyers may have little vision and aren't familiar with the history of the property. In fact, they probably don't care about its history (for example, "This is where my husband was standing when he got his big promotion.").

Hints to Buyer:

- Try to imagine the house as if it were furnished with your belongings or painted differently. If the decor is horrible, the house won't sell quickly, and you might be able to purchase it at below market price. Many ugly houses have potential to be better than the spic-and-span, dolled-up, freshly painted, sizzler homes.

- Tell your agent what you like about each home and what you do *not* like. Be truthful and thoughtful. For example, don't tell her you hate all frame houses if you hated one particular frame house because the wood was painted chartreuse. If you do, you will not see another frame house with that agent. Then, when you buy the pretty frame cottage from another agent because your original agent couldn't find anything you wanted, you will be remembered forever as a liar.

Chapter 3

Street Appeal

Budding Hollies and the Crickets

All home showings must begin on the exterior of the home; it's a logistical reality. Because of some psychological characteristic, first impressions are very important. I leave it to the heirs of Dr. Freud to tell you exactly why.

However, I can tell you that I have spent hours in debate sitting outside poorly landscaped homes with neglected lawns and enchanting interiors. During these debates, I have used all my persuasive skills in an attempt to have prospective buyers release their seatbelts and join me in a promenade through the home. Many times they won't even get out of the car.

SELLER

Sellers know their homes. They have molded and shaped them into places in which they can derive great self-satisfaction. They eat there. They sleep there. Why, they truly live there.

Sellers sometimes also have quirks. One person I know makes his wife wipe the condensation from the containers in their refrigerator. He was irritated when an agent, who evidently had soiled his hands, had the audacity to wash his hands in

11

the sink of the homeowner without toweling the droplets of water from the inside of the sink when he was finished. Yet, this same, seemingly meticulous homeowner may see no reason to waste water on a lawn or something as worthless as a holly shrub (They're not bushes. They are shrubs. One must be landscapingly correct).

Hints to Seller:

- Get the exterior perfect. Landscape. (That's a verb.)

- Go to a bait shop and buy some crickets, or, record some cricket chirps and put a speaker in the landscaping, by Jiminy.

- Work with your agent in prioritizing repairs and the expenditures within your budget. An expenditure of $200 in one area may have a return of $2,000. However, $200 spent to repair an item that has annoyed you during your stay in the house may not return a nickel. Be smart. *That'll be the day your house value skies.*

SELLER'S AGENT

Seller's agents can tell when a home needs exterior work. Ask them. They are often reluctant to tell a seller how they really feel for fear of not obtaining a listing. Sellers should let their agents know that they may critique openly and often, as long as the criticism is followed by a solution or remedy. If the property lacks street appeal, agents are tremendously handicapped in marketing the property.

It's like when you had to get your high school honey's best friend a date in order for you to go out with your honey, and the friend was as ugly as sin. No one cared that the friend had a great personality or an amazing wit or even lots of money.

Many of the seller's agent's clients (that is, those potential buyers) prefer to drive by the property prior to an actual appointment to view the property. They feel an appointment is too much of a commitment. If a residence lacks physical sizzle, buyers will not go in — no matter how hard your agent tries to persuade them. The same, of course, will be true of other agents and their clients.

Hints to Seller's Agent:

- Have an artist draw a rendering of the home with landscaping in place.

- Beg. *That'll be the day you eat humble pie.*

BUYER

The buyer's first inclination is to judge the book by its cover. As I mentioned earlier, I've tried to pry fingers loose from door handles or whatever else various buyers had found to anchor themselves with. Most buyers want to buy a house that will allow them to drive home, call all of their friends and family, boast about the beauty of the home, and gloat over their business savvy in negotiating a great deal. They don't want to be embarrassed by their purchase, and their family and pals can only see the outside. Image. Pride. Ego. Whatever you want to call it, it's there and it's a factor.

Hints to Buyer:

- Swallow your pride. This could be the deal of a lifetime. (See the final chapter.)

- Even if you don't want the all-committing "appointment," ask your agent for an information sheet and determine if the number of bedrooms, room sizes, and appliances are within the realm of your wishes. If so, go see the darn thing.

- However, beware! If a person does not properly maintain the exterior, it can lead to severe structural problems. *That'll be the day the house makes you cry.*

13

BUYER'S AGENT

Buyer's agents want to find their clients a home they will be proud of. Such a situation bodes well for the agent. Nevertheless, only on rare occasions do buyer's agents argue with a client over whether a buyer should purchase a specific house. Ruffling a buyer's feathers can lead to the buyer looking for a new realty henhouse. Buyers want direction, but very subtle direction. They are the ones that have to live with and in their home purchase.

Hints to Buyer's Agent:

- When showing a dump that could be a Shangri La, have an architect or draftsman draw some rough sketches and secure ballpark estimates from contractors for these alterations.

- Find a home that has been renovated, try to obtain before and after shots, and share them with your prospects. *That'll be the day they say they'll buy.*

Chapter 4

Non-Agent Listings

For Sale by Ogre (I mean owner)

As you know, I am a real estate agent, a REALTOR, no less. At one point in my life, I decided to delve into another business, a non-real estate venture. During that endeavor, my wife and I decided to sell our house. My real estate license was still active and I was a member of the MLS (Multiple Listing Service); however, I was not active in the real estate community. We listed our home for sale with my firm's broker as the listing agent. Why? We needed money. We needed to sell our home and retrieve the equity. We needed to net the most we possibly could.

We hired a REALTOR and agreed to pay him a six percent commission, even though I had my real estate license and access to the MLS. I could have "for sale by ownered" it, plus one notch better. But my wife and I had other jobs and we couldn't afford the sales time and effort needed to net the best results. We needed a person with his finger on the pulse of the marketplace.

One more twist was that another firm had talked to us about listing our home. Their agent had said it would be foolish to list it for over $89,000. The firm's managing broker had researched the area and concurred with her agent. I had wanted to list it

15

for $110,000, hoping to net $100,000. Their firm agreed to list it with a new agent who had "nothing else to do" for as high as $99,000. Our broker sold the house for $106,000. So the moral of the story is: Get more than one opinion.

As it turned out, my wife and I bought three houses and sold four during the next two years by using a REALTOR, when all the while I had an active license and was a member of the MLS. Our agent earned his commissions, and my wife and I earned handsome profits — simply by heeding his advice.

Who, then, would try to sell their houses themselves? Answer: only people who don't know any better.

SELLER

An owner-seller is often referred to as a FSBO (pronounced Fizzbo), acronymic for "For Sale By Owner." These people view real estate agents' car phones, sales awards, and offices as scalps on poles or notches in the grip of the gun of an old Western gunslinger. They see agents as money-sucking leeches who put a sign in the yard and wait for the check, or as underpricing con artists draining unsuspecting homeowners of the equity in their homes.

FSBOs say that agents don't give them any value for the improvements they have made on their homes. Most FSBOs want to recover every penny they have ever put into their house — even expenditures that would usually be considered a maintenance expense. Lawn care, paint, decorating, and roof repair are not investments in your home.

It's also ironic that these misers, who are trying to save a real estate commission, have overspent in almost every aspect of the home. They have a six-ton heat and air system when four tons would have worked. They paid $4,000 for ten shrubs and some monkey grass.

What's more, the sly dogs painted the house themselves. It only took them six weekends and twenty-eight weeknights, sixty gallons of paint, ten brushes, four drop cloths, three paint pans, five ruined suits, and a stained carpet. And everything's purple. (The wife saw it in *Architectural Accents*. She failed to note that the home featured was built in 1920 in downtown Baltimore. They live in a 1988 home in Suburbia, Tennessee.)

Many homes become FSBOs because the sellers had several real estate agents give them comparative market analyses and found that their home is not worth what they had hoped. So what do they do? The same thing Barney Fife did. They become real estate agents. And what usually happens? The same thing that happened to Barney Fife — their career is nipped in the bud. But not without a fight! Ogres can be very, very stubborn.

Hint to Seller:

- Get an agent.

SELLER'S AGENT

The seller's agent is the Mr. Hyde part of the ogre, with Dr. Jekyll being the seller. In the case of FSBOs, seller and seller's agent are physically one in the same, yet psychologically they are worlds apart. When showing his home, the Mr. Hyde side is unable to withstand the criticisms that unwitting, prospective buyers often utter — forgetting for that one moment that the seller's agent is, in fact, the seller himself.

Fizzboing ogres can attack without warning, usually convincing the prospect to call an agent immediately rather than deal with an ogre. For that reason, ogres are usually great for agents. Their homes can't be shown except during off hours. And usually these showings aren't really showings at all. They're more like tours, with a sales pitch — in fact, the hardest sales pitch you've ever had laid upon you.

"What's wrong with our home?" the ogre fizzboes.

"No den," the prospect buyer premises of the premises.

"Whaddya mean no den? We use this room as a den," the FSBO ogres, loudly.

"But it has a stove, dishwasher, and a refrigerator in it. It's a kitchen!" the not-this-time buyer argues.

"It's not a kitchen. It's a well-equipped, functional den. Very user friendly," the agenting owner discloses.

"We're leaving."

Hint to Seller's Agent:

- Don't Fizzbo. Get a full-time agent.

BUYER

Buyers sometimes think FSBOs are bargains. They think they are saving the real estate commissions. They pay lawyers $100 an hour to write contracts, which may not even go through. (You might recall buyer's agents usually receive compensation only when the sale closes, and often, if not most of the time, the seller will pay.)

What about a loan? Buyers generally go to their bank to get their loan. And why not? After all, that's where they have all of their accounts. But what they often don't consider is that the bank's mortgage department may not even be in the same state. They usually pay more for the loan. And what about accountability? What if the seller sort of fudges (we've had enough "lying" already) a little?

One couple I know once tried to save an $1,800 commission. They had heard they should buy FHA (that is, with a Federal Housing Administration loan). The seller (an ogre) told them they would have to pay $2,000 extra to go FHA. "It's normal," he dishonestly convinced. They paid asking price plus $2,000 for a house that he told them had "about a thousand" square feet. If 800 is about a thousand, then he told the truth. So what? Can you call the Real Estate Commission? No. He's not licensed. The Board of REALTORS? No. He's not a member. Sue him? No. They used his lawyer.

Hint to Buyer:

- Get an agent.

BUYER'S AGENT

There are times when agents must don their ogre armor and venture into Fizzboland land. It's never fun, but their clients deserve it. When all other options have failed, the agent can begin negotiations with the ogre. It is more difficult than dealing with other selling agents because the MLS information is Greek to an ogre. (Give a Fizzboer another eye and he'll be a cyclops.)

Ogres are determined not to pay a commission. They are proud to a fault, and they have drawn a line in the sand. However, the agent can and usually will prevail.

Hints to Buyer's Agent:

- Assure the ogre that you are merely an agent for a potential buyer; you're not an enemy.

- Explain the offer in a thorough, non-condescending manner. Remember: You have done this every day for years, while the ogre is trying to remember the next step in the real estate book he bought to assist him in the sale. He has never seen an adversarial agent in person. He has never negotiated a deal. Still, the ogre possesses a large ego, which needs massaging. Remember: Ogres can be transformed into humanity. After all, they do have to move somewhere. Tame them and they can be yours.

Chapter 5

Open Houses

Woodward and Bernstein Scoop Mr. and Mrs. Ida Dunn

Open Houses are seen by sellers as a one-way ticket to a sale. The owners have visions of people lining up outside their doors like fans of Bruce Springsteen and Michael Jackson during the '80s. It usually doesn't happen that way.

Woodward and Bernstein clones are usually the first on the scene as they attempt to discover the fraud being perpetrated by the sellers and their agent in a collaborative effort to sell this potentially defective dwelling for such a high price. They are interrogative with beguiling, open-ended, out-the-door, and innuendo-filled questions.

For example: "Why is the moulding behind the vanity in front of the drywall there? Is it because the vanity was an afterthought? Or is it covering a defective floor? Why are the owners moving? Is there something you're not telling us? We've been told by an anonymous source that there's a carton of expired milk in the refrigerator."

These detecting investigators are followed by the elderly Mr. and the Mrs. Ida Dunn. They are "not looking to buy, just getting ideas in case they move." The Dunns have lived in the same house for sixty-two years and paid $6,000 for 4,500 square feet. They can't believe the shortcomings of the open house.

"I mean this is all right, but you know what Ida Dunn? Ida put the shelves on this wall and the fireplace on that wall."

"And that hot jaccyousa. Heck, it's outside. Who in their right mind would ever take a bath outside? I tell you what Ida Dunn. Ida put that tub in the bathroom where it belongs."

Many times the Dunns and the Woodwards and the Bernsteins gang up on the agent and make for a long, long afternoon. I wouldn't have had that open house — know what Ida Dunn?

SELLER

The sellers, as you have learned, view their open house as the end of the sales trail. They can't imagine that the visiting tire-kickers could find anything in the house to be anything other than irresistible. They circle the house during the open house — gleefully noting the model of each car that stops and imagining the career and income of each Woodward, Bernstein, and Dunn. They make bets on which person will make the highest offer. They also go to other open houses and interrogate agents and tell them how their home is better and what theyda done.

When it's all over, they also can't believe that more people didn't attend their open house. Nor can they believe the agent didn't sell their home after they spent days cleaning and getting it ready.

Hints to Seller:

- Make the open house perfect from your end.

- Do not expect a miracle. Most listed houses are sold as a result of scheduled visits by other agents.

- Open houses are not a panacea. If agents are not showing

the home it means two things: First, they don't see it as desirable in their research and are not recommending it to their clients; and second, their clients don't feel the home is one they would like to see. Open houses do not cure overpricing, lack of street appeal, or any other shortcomings that may exist.

SELLER'S AGENT

Open houses are a necessary evil. They are a good lead source because from time to time good prospects *do* visit open houses. If this shoe doesn't fit, the agent can try the Cinderella routine. It's harder to instill loyalty in these real estatic renegades, so they must work hard and fast before the clock strikes midnight and their cars become pumpkins. Mailings, newspaper ads, prayers, proper planet alignment, and some old-fashioned luck can lead to a successful open house.

Hints to Seller's Agent:

- Have something open as often as possible. Doing so will keep you in touch with the buying market and provide you with feedback on your listings.

- Let your other clients know where your open house is when you have one. That way, they will realize you often do work seven days a week.

- Communicate. The "C" word, once again. Yet it's what most of us do worst. After having a home open, let the owners know what happened.

BUYER

Potential buyers should attend as many open houses as possible. Open houses offer a free, leisurely view of the active market, and they provide the buyers an audition ground for finding real estate. Buyers may also find the agent they wish to use as their agent when they sell. Many buyers use open houses to confirm a decision made during the previous week. Their agent has shown them several houses and they have decided upon one for which to begin negotiations. In order to assure themselves, they tour the area.

Hints to Buyer:

- Tell the agent at the open house your reason for being there.

- If you have an agent, inform the attending agent immediately upon your arrival. It can avert problems later.

- Remember things you liked and things you found offensive. You may have an open house of your own soon.

BUYER'S AGENT

Buyer's agents are probably having houses open on the same days that their buyers are on the prowl. It's unfortunate that they can't be with their clients at all times, but it is impossible. The best of agents have had clients duped by the less virtuous of the real estate agency world and no doubt lost a sale while a client bought a clunker.

Buyer's agents are confident they have shown their clients the best there is and represented them in the best way possible. However, the thought of innocent buyers out on their own is terrifying. It's not so much the fear of losing commissions or wasting time invested, though a little of that is natural and healthy. Rather it's more of a concern that the buyer will make a mistake that will require extensive work for the buyer's agent to undo, or even worse, that the buyer may purchase an atrocity that the good agent will someday have to sell.

Hints to Buyer's Agent:

- Give your clients dozens of your business cards and beg them to give them to the agents holding open houses.

- Call your clients following their open house tours to see if they did anything in which you need to become involved.

- Pray that Woodward and Bernstein don't meet Mr. and Mrs. Ida Dunn.

Open Houses

Chapter 6

Buyers

It's a Good Buy or It's Goodbye

Buyers. You gotta love 'em. They know everything. They know exactly what they want to buy and exactly what they want to spend. The only problem is they speak a language called buyerese, which is a variation of liarese.

Liarese is the language of the liars, a group of people who at times distort or twist the truth, usually for their own benefit. Buyerese, however, differs significantly from liarese insomuch as buyers are really *trying* to tell the truth. For some reason, though, when people begin looking for a house, the truthful needs and impulses swimming around in their vast, neurological ocean somehow don't flow into their vocal chords. To the untrained observer, it would seem that these people are liars. But they're not really liars — at least not on purpose. They're simply buyers.

I have some dear friends who returned to Nashville after having lived in another city for several years. He's a lawyer and she's an architect. Now, it might seem that they wouldn't require a real estate agent because, between the two of them, they should know everything. Nevertheless, they couldn't find the house they wanted, so they asked me to assist them in their search.

At our first meeting, they informed me of the criteria required to home them. They had a young child, so they didn't want to be on a busy street. As a gauge they decided against any property on a street that was decorated with a double yellow (no passing) line. She had designed a number of homes and was partial to frame construction, although brick would be considered. They did not want stone. They refused to live on a corner lot. They wanted all the living area on one floor and did not want to spend over $125,000.

It was immediately very obvious to a person schooled in buyerese translation why they had been unable to find their dream home. They were speaking buyerese and didn't know it.

Where are they now? I'm happy to report that they are happily settled in their new home. It is a beautiful one-and-a-half-story stone home with a basement (three floors) − all comfortably situated on a corner lot bounded by a street with a double yellow line. And they paid $126,000 for it.

BUYER

Once you get past the language barrier, you find that buyers really are good people. And some actually do, in fact, truly know their quest. (The above example is extreme, though still true. Every REALTOR has three stories just like it.) Many buyers think they know what they want, but really haven't approached enough houses from a buyer's perspective to be able to contrast and compare the infinite number of possibilities available.

Buyers often are intimidated. They are swimming in uncharted waters, armed only with horror stories from friends and bits and pieces of information garnered from newspaper articles, late-night television promotions, and a "how to" book. More often than not, they are unable to differentiate between a well-built, nicely designed, functional, messy home and a clean, shiny, meticulous, structually hazardous, choppy, nonfunctional dwelling.

28

Many times buyers will worry more about roof color than roof condition. And common settlement cracks scare them to death.

Hints to Buyer:

- Begin your hunt very open-minded. Cull as you go.

- Try to remember why you want the things you do. The reasons may be trivial.

- Explain to your agent why you don't like a particular house you visit. Doing so will allow the agent to rethink your case.

- There's no reason to be embarrassed about changing your mind. Many times after seeing several homes, you realize you were completely wrong about what you wanted. Change is good. *You* are going to have to live there. Tell your agent.

- Never lie or speak buyerese. If you can't stand a particular home, tell your agent (even if she is the one listing it).

- Don't be afraid to find the house you want. When you find it, buy it — even it it's the first house you see.

BUYER'S AGENT

Normally, a potential buyer is referred to the agent or vice versa. The agent then meets with the buyer to determine the financial capabilities of the buyer, sometimes called pre-qualifying. (I fail to see what is so "pre" about it.) The agent sees what price home the prospects would be able to purchase. The prospects then define, to the best of their ability, their dream home.

The buyer's agent is just that...an agent. He is not going to pitch any homes. He will run a CMA (remember...Comparative Market Analysis) to determine if the home is priced within the realm of acceptibility. He will point out benefits and features, as well as deficiencies. Price range often eliminates some areas, and the agent must then search the remaining areas for homes that meet the standards set by the prospective buyers.

Next comes the showing mission. The first few days are devoted to exhibitionary expeditions that familiarize the buyer with the territory and natures of the beasts in the realty wilderness. Then the short list is made. At this time, spouses or significant others join in on the fun. Pencils are sharpened, ballpark figures for financing turn into estimates, and magnifying glasses appear. The word "contract" (gulp) is used. Then the experts are called. (See next chapter.)

Hints to Buyer's Agent:

- Listen.

- Translate what buyers are saying into what they mean.

- Be thorough with your comparable sales and financial representations.

- Don't be afraid to give buyers a subtle push if they find the right home. Sometimes they're begging for it.

- Keep 'em happy.

SELLER

Sellers should view buyers as their friends. They are the people for whom the sellers have waited and toiled. Every person who sees the home is not a buyer. There will be only one. Every home has its good features, along with several characteristics that might prove negative to some people. Most homes have flexibility but are not structural chameleons with the ability to change to suit the lifestyles of every person.

Sellers should not talk to the buyers prior to closing. Although they speak buyerese, the sellers' every word will be held against them at a later date. Realize, too, that if prospect traffic is good through the home, but no buyer surfaces, the house is not a good buy.

Hints to Seller:

- If you priced your house too high in hopes of gaining an unusually large profit and the house hasn't sold in two months, reduce the price. When you reduce the price, put a "Reduced" sign on your "For Sale" sign. Otherwise, John Q. Public will be unaware of the reduction. It does not reflect a "fire sale" attitude on your behalf. It is reduced. It's for sale. Let drivers-by know it.

- Try to view your home objectively as a buyer. Clear your mind, drive to a real estate office, and then drive back to your home and pretend you are a prospective buyer. See how it looks as you approach and how easy it is to enter. Sticking locks or squeaky, inoperable doors present an image of more inoperable things to follow. Walk through each room as you would someone else's home. View it through a visitor's eyes. Open your senses. Sniff. Are there any smells unique to your home? If so, lose them. Trust your nose. It knows.

A sound analogy: In the multi-million dollar recording studios in Nashville, after all the tracks are laid and engineers have spent hours upon hours getting each note of every instrument and each voice mixed perfectly while listening on zillion-dollar sound systems, they flip a switch to see how the song will sound on a cheap car radio. That is where the decision is made. The song must pass the test of the keen ear of the engineer, but the not-necessarily keen ear of the consumer is what matters most.

The same applies to your home. The little details are great, but don't forget the basics. If your house smells, your neighbor's sells.

SELLER'S AGENT

The seller's agent must work with the seller to make the property as easy to show as possible. The property should be priced competitively, be easy to show, and be free of any petzillas or their reminders, as well as free of any glaring deficiencies. The seller's agent must cooperate with other agents and agencies in the sale of the property and use every resource available to transform prospects into buyers. They will arrange the showings, open houses, inspections, contract negotiations, appraisals, and closing. Only then do they get paid.

Hints to Seller's Agent:

- Make the property showable.
- Make the property sellable.
- Make the seller negotiate.
- Work it till you drop.
- Make it a good buy or it's goodbye.

Chapter 7

The Parent Trap

Ma and Pa Meddle

In many cases, prior to finalizing the purchase of their home, the buyers want their parents to inspect the property. The buyers have not heeded a word of advice from their parents since they were eleven years old, but now, following twenty-something years of arguments and disagreements, they want the folks to share in the biggest decision of their lives.

Personally, I would prefer an inspection team comprised of Felix Unger, Frank Lloyd Wright, and Sherlock Holmes to that of a parental pair, especially if the parents are divorced. The "see who can find the most wrong" game begins.

The parents have not lived with their children since the kids were in high school. They think their kids still leave their retainers on the sink and pop pimples onto the mirror. It follows then that they must know exactly what their children want and need to fit their Neverneverland lifestyles.

It's even more alarming when the parents are not familiar with the market. They are astounded at the prices and, oh, the interest rates. The monthly payment amount brings an expression of shock, pain, and disbelief. How in the world can their little boy or girl afford such an expense! The poor kid makes barely $2 a day selling lemonade on the corner. Most parents in this situation haven't shopped for a home in over twenty years and can't fathom a thirty-year mortgage. All that interest!

And don't let the parental eyeglasses fool you. They are just a prop. These wonderful people can spot a nail hole from seventy feet and through two sets of windows. They can hear a floor squeak at a noise level that is only audible to bats. Not only that, but they are upset with the real estate agent for trying to make their children spend more than they can afford, while repaying an exorbitant loan at usurious interest rates on an overpriced property.

If the property is newly constructed, the old adage, "They sure don't make them like they used to," is always heard. While on older properties, the saying is, "Son, you could get a brand new house for less than they want for this old thing."

Generally speaking, however, the real problem lies in that they want the best for their children, and their children simply can't afford the best. No one wishes they were buying a bigger home more than the REALTOR, but facts are facts, and this is it. Parents are not shy either. The "Have you seen this?!" cry usually echoes down the hallway at least five times prompting a race to the source of the utterance. Usually the great horror turns out to be a very minor defect like, say, a leaky faucet.

BUYER

The buyers feel their parents are better qualified to make this decision since the folks have done it before. Never mind that their homes were purchased when an ARM was just an appendage attached to the shoulder, not an adjustable rate mortgage. Building codes were more relaxed in the past and deficiencies were grandfathered in. They don't make them like they used to. Of course they don't. It's illegal!

But young buyers want Ma and Pa to approve — just as they brought their prospective spouse home for the first time. The parents never feel the fiance' is good enough either, but they finally (usually) accept the new spouse. And they will do the same with the house.

Hints to Buyer:

- Honor thy father and thy mother...after you buy the house. Honor thy agent and thy inspector and thy own good judgment prior to that. You're the one that has looked at seventy-two houses trying to find the right one. You've had your agent run the comparable sales and the mortgage numbers, while shopping rates from California to Sweden. The inspector has donned his coveralls and crawled over, under, and through every inch.

- Give your folks a hug, put them in their car, smile, and wave. Walk back into the house and sign the contract.

BUYER'S AGENT

The buyer's agent has done all she can do and is now at the mercy of highly subjective, usually underinformed persons. The agent must present only facts and not appear to be at all determined to make the home pass this particular inspection. Additionally, the agent must reinforce the offspring's decision to purchase. Comparable sales quotations, financial information, and references to any inspection that might have been performed should be shared with the parents.

In short, the parents must be provided with all the information the child had when it made the decision. Forget that the agent has spent sixty hours with the potential buyer, has years in the business, and has done hours of research in order to get the deal to this position. He still must share all of his accumulated knowledge and data with the parents in thirty minutes — all while not appearing to be biased. It is a challenge that approaches the impossible.

Hints to Buyer's Agent:

- Let Ma and Pa Meddle.

- Reinforce their ideas when they are accurate. Thank them for their insight in areas you might have missed, and admit you missed them.

- Correct the parents (gently, gently!) when they are wrong, and do so respectfully and with the parents and buyers together.

- Roll with the punches. Thicken your skin. Smile.

SELLER

Sellers usually feel they have been persecuted and tormented throughout the months the house was on the market, beaten during contract negotiations, and accused by an inspection. And now. Now they have to hope their house appeals to people who will probably visit it two or three times a year for the next six years. I have never seen "subject to parental approval" as a condition of a contract, but it might as well be.

Hints to Seller:

- Leave the house and go look at the place you're moving into.

- Have *your* parents inspect the house *you* are buying. If that's not possible, borrow the parents of one of your friends. It has the same effect.

SELLER'S AGENT

The seller's agent has done everything required to get the situation to this point, and he will do everything needed to overcome this predictable obstacle. He has seen enough parental inspections to know how to advise the seller, and he can work with the buyer's agent to determine if any pre-parent preparation should be taken.

Hints to Seller's Agent:

- Have the home accessible for people whose age could reach the nineties. The parents are usually in better shape than I am, but sometimes age has brought its common hindrances. Be alert and sensitive to any special needs.

- Ask the other agent if you need to be present for the parental showing, but make every effort to avoid attending. Two agents can seem like a gang.

- Give them the key and let Ma and Pa Meddle.

Chapter 8

The Offer

The Greedledees Meet the Greedledums

The sellers have called their agent repeatedly begging for action. They really need to sell their home. They are moving or they have found the perfect home. Bring them an offer...anything. Make somebody do something.

The prospects who saw the sellers' house loved it. It has everything they could ever want and more. The price is right. Interest rates are right. Venus is aligned with Mars. This deal should be simple to put together, right? Wrong!

This is where the Greedledees meet the Greedledums. Davy Crockett had it easy at the Alamo compared to what's in store for these combatants. It doesn't have to be that way.

BUYER

The buyers have looked at many, many homes. They have defined and redefined their goals. Of everything they have seen, this home is the best. They knew the price when they walked in. Their agent has supplied them with a CMA that should establish the value of the home. They have slept on it, prayed over it, run the numbers, put a pencil to it, asked Ma and Pa, and they have only one more question:

"What did the sellers pay for it?"

"What difference does it make? They bought it thirty years ago?" the agent ponders aloud.

"We just wonder?"

"They paid $62,000."

"AND THEY WANT $97,000?!"

Never mind that the price is actually very reasonable based on comparable sales. Never mind that it is better suited for their needs than any home currently on the market. You have just met the Greedledees.

In an effort to try to make her spouse enter the realm of realty reality, the less greedy of the pair asks: "What do you think they have in it?" This question refers to the monetary total of the improvements contained within the home. They hope this amount will be $35,000 or more. That way the seller is, at best, breaking even, and maybe even LOSING MONEY. The mere thought of a seller's loss brings a gleam to the eyes of the Greedledees. They clasp each other's hands. They want to boast of their financial conquest to Ma and Pa. ("Look, Ma, no hands!")

Yes, the Greedledees want blood! They will not sleep if the seller is able to sleep. (By the way, the Greedledees met their agent at church.)

"Let's offer $50,000," the Greedledees grumble.

Now would be a wonderful time for a recitation of the Beatitudes or the Golden Rule, or a simple, "Why the heck did you even look at homes in this price range if you're going to offer this?" But patience is a REALTOR's virtue. So he will tell you:

Hints to Buyer:

- What the seller paid for it is of little consequence.

- What the seller "has in it" is of little consequence.

- A horribly low offer will not save you money or get you a deal. In fact, it will probably cost you later.

- Prioritize. If price is your main concern, forgo nagging contingencies. If not, add as many as you like. (Examples include: financing, structural, HVAC, electrical, plumbing, repairs, and allowances.)

- You can catch more homes with sweet, reasonable offers than you can with sour, low-ball ones.

BUYER'S AGENT

The buyer's agents have spent hours setting appointments and showings, researching every angle, and basically tending to the whims of the Greedledees. It seemed odd that they were looking for a $100,000 home when they dressed in garage sale clothes, but nevertheless their financial situation justified it. They seemed so subdued and congenial during the various showings.

Hints to Buyer's Agent:

- Beware of wolves in cheap clothing.

- Use comparable sales, this book, anything you can to get the first offer into the non-abrasive zone.

- Warn the other agent and beg for a counter.

- Don't try to justify the unjustifiable. If your offer is too low, do not try to convince the other agent that the property is overpriced.

- Warn your buyers that neither God nor the Constitution of the United States nor the Bill of Rights nor any other amendment guarantees individuals "the right to negotiate."

- Give your client a chance to get a good deal.

SELLER

An offer is a piece of paper. It cannot harm anyone. If it is too low, a counter offer should be made. No one has to accept an offer. There's no reason for anyone to become overly angry or upset. It is a start and it's better than what was there prior to the offer.

Unfortunately, many sellers see the offer as a line drawn in the sand or a call to battle stations. A war is on. They want asking price. ("This house is perfect. It's better than the one down the street that sold for less.") The offer is the first step toward attaining the goal set when the house was put on the market. And yet the offer is often unappreciated, even despised.

Hints to Seller:

- The buyers think they have a God-given "right to negotiate." Give it to 'em.

- Remember the CMA and your agent's initial visit. If the agent is suggesting you take less than the CMA, remind him. If you *are* getting what the agent projected, accept it.

- Try to purge the offer of unnecessary clauses or conditions in order that you and the buyer can reduce any gap to only appreciable differences.

- The potential buyers may not be much, but they're all you've got right now. Try to keep the deal alive.

- If the buyers offer to pay you for your house, you aren't "giving it away."

SELLER'S AGENT

The sellers have bemoaned the lack of an offer for days, weeks, sometimes months. Their agent has tried every trick in the book to get even a nibble. Yet, when a fish finally takes the bait and the agent brings an offer to the home of the seller, things change.

The sellers can't imagine why their agent is so excited. Whose side is the agent on? This offer stinks. If it were cheese, it would be limburger. The sellers want to make it Swiss. All this talk of food has made them hungrier still. They decide to keep their stove and refrigerator even though they already have six. The Greedledums have come home. Maybe for good.

Hints to Seller's Agent:

- Separate the contract into sections; important, unimportant; affects their net, doesn't affect their net; normal conditions, abnormal conditions.

- Remind them of the CMA.

- Give them a chance to get a deal. Counter and test the water (if it's within realty reality).

- Represent the best interests of your clients even if they don't agree with you.

Warning to Greedledees and Greedledums

John Lennon wrote and recorded a song titled "Instant Karma." Most listeners are unaware that it's a song written about real estate. If you greedle, "instant karma's gonna get you." If a Greedledee becomes obsessed with hurting the seller and greedles him to the point of no return, the seller will eventually refer the 'dee to another piece of real estate — the pavement.

If the Greedledee has not negotiated in good faith, instant karma occurs. That Greedlebuyer will never, ever see a deal as good as the one that he let greedle away...and, the seller will get a better offer than that of the Greedledee.

Likewise, instant karma can hit Greedledums. If they greedle would-be buyers away, the buyers will 'dee-terminate. In layman's terms, they will not be back, and the 'dummies will never see an offer as good as the one they refused.

If you are a buyer and you fail to reach an agreement with a seller because of his Greedledumness, fear not. Instant karma is with thee always. You will get an even better deal down the road.

Chapter 9

The Sale

The Sacrificial Lamb

Both buyer and seller have greedled to their heart's discontent. They have described each other in words that would make Eddie Murphy blush. They have insinuated that their agents are carpetbagging weasels. They have totally forgotten the reason the entire operation was undertaken in the first place: the sale of a piece of real estate.

Both parties have countered and recountered and recountered and decountered. They have decided they love things that they formerly abhorred and that they could care less for things that seemed to be so dear to them only hours ago. Suddenly, in a gesture that would make Mother Teresa seem selfish, one party accepts the counter of the other. Only to be nice. Not because it is a good deal. Not because the other party has negotiated in good faith and sacrificed a great deal. And certainly not because either agent has done anything of merit.

Rather, it is because the acceptor is the redeemer, the chosen one, sent by God to bestow riches upon the party of the second part. Hallelujah! The counterers also feel that the counter proposed was a bit too high, but for the good of the world of real estate, they have offered themselves as a living sacrifice.

When the appropriate Greedle accepts the counter-counter-counter, there is no joy in Greedleville. You see, now they know one thing for sure: They offered too much. Hence the real estate agent's paradoxical dilemma, Greedledees think if Greedledums accept their counter, then they countered too high. Greeeledums think if the 'dees accept their counter, they countered too low.

Therefore in Greedlese, the perfect counter offer is one that is not acceptable. But if neither party accepts a counter, there is no sale. So one Greedle must make the ultimate sacrifice. It is a far, far better thing than they have ever done before.

BUYER

Buyers cannot believe they are paying this much for that house. It is higher than they had told their respective selves they would go. (Yes, they don't mean to, but they even lie to themselves.) They have also tried to convince their agent that they will not go above a certain price.

Oddly enough, the house was listed for more than that amount, and they still couldn't wait to see it. They even called the listing agent in case their own agent was unable to drop every single thing she was doing to let them see this wonderful prize of a home. Sadly, sometimes buyers stubbornly insist that they won't pay more than, for example, ninety percent of the listing price, even though the wiser buying spouse realizes the fairness of the seller's offer.

Many times, buyers lose the home of their dreams over a couple of thousand dollars, which in buyer's terms equates to $17-$24 a month for the length of their residence, which is usually less than seven years. (That's $1,800 spread over eighty-four months). Tsk. Tsk. Instant karma's gonna get them.

Hints to Buyer:

- Carpe Dealem. Seize the deal. Fight for the best deal on the best house. When you have it, seize it.

- "Pride comes before a fall" ("I'm a Loser" — Lennon/McCartney)

- "Instant karma's gonna get you" ("Instant Karma" — John Lennon)

- If the house will appraise for contract price, you have not paid too much. If you have a financing contingency, the house must appraise.

- "Don't worry. Be happy." (Bobby McFerrin)

BUYER'S AGENT

The buyer's agent becomes least appreciated at this point of the game. The agent has shown the buyers thousands of square feet of construction and acre upon acre of land. He has exhausted every resource available — from the multi-million-dollar Multiple Listing Service to the thirty-five-cent area newspaper — in an effort to represent the buyers in the most efficient and effective manner possible.

Now, buyer (Greedledee) and buyer's agent have agreed that they (that's teamwork for you) have found the right place. They have made an offer and a counter offer. They have danced around the real-estatic floor. It's time to pay the fiddler. Now, the agent must become the heavy. The deal is a good one — statistically speaking, aesthetically thinking, and functionally programming. Yet, to the buyer, it is still the ultimate sacrifice to accept the counter offer.

Hints to Buyer's Agent:

- Arm yourself with data. Just the facts ma'am. No time for intangibles here.

- Conjure and evoke memories of homes less attractive.

- Appreciate the buyer's position. Be nice.

- If it is a good deal, say so. Real estate is your profession. Stand by your land.

- Remind the 'dees that $2,000 is $2,000 to the seller, but only a few dollars per month to them.

- Thank them for their sacrifice.

SELLER

The sellers placed their home on the market, never dreaming of the inconveniences, hard work, and embarassment involved. Their home has been invaded by these ETs (Equity Thieves) during every hour of the day. Then some ETs return for a second visit...and a third. Then they want to bring their parents. (Don't believe it? Go back to Chapter 7.) "These prospects must love it!! They'll pay anything!" the Greedles begin to dum. All this work will finally reward them, they think.

Then comes the offer.

And thus cometh the War of the Worlds. After a valiant effort, the Homelings realize the advanced weaponry from the ETs is too formidable for their protective shield, i.e., their agent. So they surrender. Chances are, they received more than the CMA projected, but it's an empty, hollow victory.

Hints to Seller:

- Prepare for a battle with the ETs and plan it.

- Take the second best price for the CMA if it is actually comparable to your home and has closed within the last ninety days. Use that price per square foot as your goal.

- Play not to lose, not to win. Then you won't and you will.

SELLER'S AGENT

The seller's agent has had an open house, networked with other agents, mailed fliers, advertised in newspapers, buried a statue of Saint Joseph, placed the home in the MLS, and done all kinds of other things to bring this moment to being.

This buyer is the one. No one else in the whole, wide world wants the house at this point. The sellers need to sell their house for a fair price. Still, the sellers suggest the agent is out for a commission, not their best interests. Hogwash! Reputation is more important than any individual sale.

Hints to Seller's Agent:

- Let the sellers say five mean things to you without debating or defending. On the sixth, defend your point.

- Make the sale happen. The first offer is usually from the eventual buyer. Keep it alive.

- Don't expect thanks. They usually don't come. But you should still count your blessings.

The Sale

Chapter 10

The Inspection

The Dealslayer

Ma and Pa have meddled. The Greedledees have greedled the Greedledums. The ETs (Equity Thieves) have pillaged and plundered the ogres. Ida and her old man have Dunn the house in and Woodward and Bernstein have tongue-depressed their deepest throat. It is now time for the inspector.

The inspector arrives with a flashlight, coveralls, a ladder, and a clipboard equipped with a form that lists all the possible deficiencies of a house. The form also has a disclaimer stating that the house could fall into the earth two seconds after the inspector's departure and that he can't be held accountable because, after all, he's just an inspector and is therefore unable to see into the future.

Some home inspectors hate houses and attack them with a vengeance — noting every settlement crack, nail pop, paint chip, and squeaky faucet. They may note a cracked plynth block on the report, or even a crack in the flitch beam. Flitch beam. Plynth block. It's all Greek to the buyer. One buyer might freak over a cracked plynth block, while another might not flinch at a cracked flitch. Plynths are decorative. Flitch beams are structural. There is a huge difference.

The buyer should be informed as to what is major and what

is not. By noting meaningless trivialities, the inspector may cause the buyer to fail to realize a real problem. A few home inspectors feel they are there to slay the dragon (with the deal being the dragon).

An inspector may have been a builder in another life during which no one bought his spec houses. He may have a vendetta against real estate agents. And some inspectors simply like to scare people. Remember when you were little and people told ghost stories? Some home inspectors tell house stories with the same motive. Others try to impress you with their keen knowledge of construction, engineering, and even areas that don't pertain to houses — for example, international finance, European culture, and extraterrestrial life.

Good inspectors arrive and ask questions before providing answers. "What am I looking for?" or "What are your concerns?" With an understanding established, they will point out areas that may be either a huge problem or just a minor flaw that the buyers might want to address at some point during their occupation of the residence.

BUYER

Buyers are scared to death that they are making a mistake. Buyer's remorse is a very real psychological state into which most buyers enter. The inspection is a monumental occasion that can provide great relief, satisfaction, and justification. Their homeful hopes hinge on the outcome of this exercise performed by this perilous expert. They will believe every word the inspector says and even some he does not.

If the inspector says, "The roof looks like it's about five or six years old," buyers don't realize that means it should last another ten or fifteen years. They hear "the roof is old and must be replaced immediately." Buyers also frequently think the cost of a new roof is much greater than it really is.

Hints to Buyer:

- The inspector is the expert. You are not supposed to know anything about construction. If the inspector makes a comment that you don't understand, ask for an explanation. You're paying for that information.

- Have your agent be present to interpret and advise in case an issue arises.

- The inspection should not be a top secret, subversive plot to kill the deal. It is an informative experience. Allow the homeowner to be present. There may be a logical explanation for a puzzling circumstance.

- Don't let a cracked plynth block kill the deal.

BUYER'S AGENT

The agent for the buyer usually arranges the inspection. The agent has experience in this field and is familiar with the various inspectors and their modus operandi. Contrary to what most Greedles think, both agents hope the inspector finds a flaw if there is a flaw to be found. It is most embarrassing to an agent to have represented a buyer in the purchase of a defective home. For that reason, buyers should gave great faith in the inspector recommended by their agent, but should ask for the names and phone numbers of several inspectors and then make their own choice.

Hints to Buyer's Agent:

- Get a thorough inspector. Offer several to the buyers, or refer them to the yellow pages.

- Explain the comments of the inspector to the buyers while on the site. Settlement cracks seem to enlarge in the minds of the buyers after they leave.

- Explain which items are the responsibility of the seller

and which are the responsibility of the buyer. Ask the inspector for an estimated cost to repair any items that the buyer will have to repair (even if you already know).

SELLER

Sellers usually worry themselves sick over the inspection — at times, rightfully so. Many states are now requiring sellers to disclose any known defects when they sell their homes. These laws will greatly increase the income of attorneys in those states because proving a person knew about a defect can be difficult. Many times, things break that the seller simply didn't know were defective. That's the reason for the inspection. In fact, problem situations generally have been addressed prior to putting the home on the market.

Hints to Seller:

- Don't try to hide the shortcomings of your home. A plant over a carpet stain or a cloth over a cracked commode top will cause the inspector to reach for his fine-toothed comb.

- If you are asked to leave the premises during the inspection, leave any warranties, as well as receipts for any repairs that you have had done while in your home.

- Don't worry. If it ain't broke, you don't have to fix it.

SELLER'S AGENT

The agent for the seller must learn the name of the inspector and seek background information on this person. Every effort should be made to attend the inspection in order to defend the home. There are vengeful inspectors out there. Dealslayers, in fact. They have pictures on their walls and have mounted shingles with the addresses of their kills engraved on copper tubing.

The seller's agent should be thoroughly familiar with the house and able to answer questions posed by the inspector. In the event that Monsieur Clouseau has decided that the sellers (who are not to be confused with Clouseau himself, oui?) should not partake in the inspectacle, the seller's agent should arrange to have the sellers in a telephonically accessible location so that they can provide any needed information.

Hints to Seller's Agent:

- Do a Superman imitation — fight for truth, justice, and the American way.

- If it's broke, somebody's gotta fix it. Determine who will fix it and when *at the inspection.*

- If you smell a dealslayer early in the inspection, call for reinforcements. Ask your own inspector or a builder to look at the perceived problems.

- If problems persist, remind the dealslayer of another Cooper novel, *The Last of the Mohicans.* The word "Mohican" means home inspector.

Chapter 11

The Mortgage

Little House on the Variable

When Charles Ingalls built his little house in Walnut Grove, he didn't have to worry about a mortgage. As he accumulated monies, he purchased materials and added on. Now, the Japanese have one-hundred-year mortgages, and American homebuyers can shop at a mortgage company in a manner similar to choosing cantaloupes. You can thump and thump until one feels right.

For example, you can thump ARMs, which are adjustable rate mortgages. An ARM can adjust annually or every three years or at the end of five years or even at the end of seven. Some adjust twice a year. In any case, the borrower is at the mercy of the market and the anniversary date of his particular ARM. Timing is everything.

In 1990, rates were fairly stable all year until Saddam Hussein invaded Kuwait. That day the rates shot up so fast that a Patriot missile could not have intercepted them. Rates stayed high for several days until President Bush sent the troops over and the nation became sortie friendly and realized this was nothing to lose interest over. The rates returned to normal.

However, the borrowers whose loan anniversaries happened to fall during those four days when rates soared o'er the ramparts had to live with those rates for another year. Four days out of three hundred and sixty-five the rates were high. It probably cost thousands of borrowers, millions of dollars. For that reason, if you are going to have a house on a variable rate, make it a *little* house on a variable.

BUYER

Buyers need to be aware that, although the institutions that share their money with borrowers are called lenders, they can be divided into four subgroups: benders, menders, penders, and renders.

Benders comply with all federal regulations, but give the buyer, who is now also the borrower, the benefit of the doubt. Fannie Mae is the Federal National Mortgage Association and has more guidelines than the Constitution. The courts interpret the Constitution in all sorts of ways — some liberal, some conservative. Benders feel that FNMA (Fannie Mae) can be interpreted in different ways, too, and they are correct.

Benders are usually found in the person of the mortgage loan officer, who is sometimes referred to as an originator, for he originates the loan. Some should be called terminators. Individuality plays a large role here. The lending world is no different from the rest of the world. Some are slackers, and others are diligent brain-rackers.

The menders are originators who can repair bad credit. Not everyone who has bad credit deserves a bad rap. At times, there are logical explanations for bad credit. Fannie Mae is a forgiving woman. She can be convinced that the borrower is contrite and should be absolved of any past sins. Mending involves more work, which is why many people in the lending ranks turn their flanks to bad credit.

The penders are usually folks who want to be benders but lack the smarts, or who try to mend but lack the gumption. They collect all the necessary documentation, quote good rates, but somehow cannot manage to close the loan. The interest rates can only be locked for sixty days, but the deal is not yet approved. They always need one more thing. There have been times when penders have taken three months and still not gotten an approval.

Last, we meet the renders. They take one look at the sales price, the credit report, and the borrowers and then begin to gnash their teeth, beat their chests, pour dirt on their heads, and rend their clothes. The only loans they want are no-brainers — for example, people who have $5 million in the bank, have worked for the same employer for ten years, and want to borrow $30,000.

Hints to Buyer:

- Let your agent guide you through the borrowing process. Rates and discount points aren't everything. You may be quoted half a point lower by a pender and end up paying a higher interest rate with a bender six months later.
- Ask the lender for a recent reference.
- Have your information ready — i.e., all loans, account numbers, addresses, places of residence, landlords, mortgage companies, places of employment, their addresses, tax returns, pay stubs, etc.
- "Truth in Lending" statements are lies.
- "Good Faith Estimates" are not.

BUYER'S AGENT

The buyer's agent usually has a "pet" originator/loan officer. This agent and lender team have joined forces to pull through borrowers whom renders rended or penders pended. They have fought Ms. Fannie Mae while bending like a tree in a hurricane or mending like a seamstress on the battlefield. The buyer's agent knows which financing program will work for this deal. Should the seller pay some points? Should the buyer go conventional or FHA (Federal Housing Administration)? The mortgage loan safari is a trip through thick forest that intimidates, humiliates, and often infuriates the borrower.

Hints to Buyer's Agent:

- Make the buyers aware of every avenue of financing available. Let them know why you feel they should go the way you propose.

- Warn the buyers about penders and renders.

- Describe the loan application in great detail. Have the buyers prepared.

- Attend the loan application with them. Loan people often make statements that scare buyers to death.

- Warn the buyers that a "truth in lending" statement is not ever the truth and that a "good faith estimate" is really a hedge against a lawsuit if the lender really blows it.

SELLER

The sellers are relieved they have found a buyer for their house. They have survived the War of the Worlds and all that preceded it. But, as Yogi Berra once said, "It ain't over till it's over." The method of purchase may have ramifications for the seller.

If the home is being purchased with a loan guaranteed by FHA, it must meet certain structural and cosmetic criteria. Unless it is stated otherwise, the seller is responsible for the costs incurred completing these repairs. Loans guaranteed by the Veterans Administration require the seller to pay all discount points. Likewise, Fannie Mae may ask you to have your dwelling conform to local building codes.

Hints to Seller:

- Have your agent explain your responsibilities associated with the loan that the buyer is attempting to obtain.

- If the buyer is assuming your loan, have the lender explain the potential of your liability. You don't want to end up with two little houses on the variable.

- After the credit report and deposit verifications are in the lender's hands, a determination can be made as to the likelihood of the loan being granted. If everything is in order, relax.

SELLER'S AGENT

The seller's agent will learn from the buyer's agent exactly with whom the buyer will apply for a loan. At the appropriate time, the seller's agent will communicate with the lender to see if there should be any concern. The lender cannot divulge specifics of the loan and will not breach the confidentiality boundaries. But, if all is well in Lendingland, that information may be passed on.

The seller's agent may want to meet the appraiser to ensure that the appraiser is aware of the comparable sales on which the agent based the sales price. From time to time, an agent can help an appraiser understand the value of a home. Appraisers are always open for sales information because that allows them to provide the best service.

Hints to Seller's Agent:

- Communicate with the buyer's agent.

- Communicate with the lender.

- Meet the appraiser at the home. Be prepared to assist in her work.

- Keep your sellers informed. Prepare them for the road ahead.

Chapter 12

The Closing

More Like the Cloning...of Eddie Haskell

By the time the closing rolls around — and it does — all four combatants (buyer and buyer's agent, seller and seller's agent) are fit to be tied. The sellers have told their agent that they hope their house caves in on the buyer and the buyer's agent immediately following the closing.

The buyers can't believe the sellers have denied them unlimited access to their future home over the past several days. What a flimsy excuse to disallow admittance...they were packing to move. The agents have made every attempt to shield their clients from the shrapnel flying from inspectorial explosions and financial institutional blasts. Both sides fear a dogfight as the buyers and sellers meet to close the deal.

Both agents warn their clients. "The water is under the bridge," "don't burn any bridges," and other bridge analogies have been offered as the agents hope themselves to be bridges over troubled waters. The buyers and their agent and the sellers and their agent arrive. Suddenly, a strange metamorphosis occurs and the buyers and sellers become Eddie Haskells.

"Hello, Mr. Seller. Isn't it a lovely day?" the buyer offers. "I hope we will be able to maintain the wonderful standard of

quality of life that you have so tremendously manifested during
your residency."

"Oh, you're too kind. We just hope we have left the home in
a condition worthy of your inhabitance," the seller Haskells.
"By the way, we left that refrigerator for you...kind of a
housewarming gift."

"Sheesh!" both agents punctuate with rolling eyes.

BUYER

The closing is the closing. Once closed, it cannot be
reopened. The documentation is written in legalese and will be
paraphrased by the closing attorney or an agent of the closing
attorney. Most of the forms conform to govermental
guidelines, and the language contained within the body of the
documentation cannot be changed or amended — even if the
buyer does not agree with it. The numbers, however are supplied by the lender. The lender, be it a bender, mender, or
render can make a mistake. Many have, many times.

Hints to Buyer:

- If you feel you should read every word of every document
  you sign, get a copy the day prior to closing. Ask questions
  then, not at closing. The closing agent may not have the
  knowledge to answer all questions.

- Compare the figures disclosed to you in the truth-in-
  lending statement to those on the closing statement. If
  they differ greatly, either way, ask the question. Even if
  the error seems to be in your favor, the head-in-the-sand
  tactic won't make it go away. It could haunt you later.

- The attorney and your agent are being paid for their
  work. If you have a question, ask now, or forever hold
  your piece (of property).

- If your parents are so inclined, this is a great time to let Ma and Pa Meddle.

BUYER'S AGENT

The buyer's agent coordinates the closing with the buyer, the seller's agent, the lender, and the closing attorney. The agent will assist the buyer in obtaining documents that are conditions of the closing. These conditions could include termite letters, notice of completion forms, inspection releases, etc.

Despite the thoroughness and preparation by all parties, problems can still surface prior to the closing. For example, a problem could arise from a reinspection, at which time a defect is noticed that was missed at the first inspection. Or termites could suddenly appear. Or maybe a loan question comes up for error. Just remember: These bugs (literally, maybe) can be resolved.

Hints to Buyer's Agent:

- You have been here before. Try to get a copy of the closing statement and pertinent financial data in advance. Check everything from the address to the tax proration.

- Follow up in a couple of weeks to ensure the recorded deed and title insurance policy have arrived. (Normally, the title insurance commitment is given at closing.)

- Try to go over the statement prior to closing. Tensions are running at a fever pitch during most closings.

- Know your stuff.

SELLER

This is the magical moment that the sellers have long awaited —the reward for the valor they exhibited in the face of the enemy. They hope the bottom line is not a surprise. Common surprises: The survey may show a driveway encroaches upon an adjoining property. A mechanic's lien may have been filed by the plumbingly inept, but legally expert plumber, whom the seller would not pay because the plumber did not complete the work to the seller's satisfaction. Maybe the mortgage balance was higher than expected, or there may have been a shortage in the escrow account. Yikes!

Hints to Seller:

- Get the closing information as early as possible in order to clear up glitches. There could be a delinquent taxpayer with your name who has caused Fannie Mae's uncle, Uncle Sam, to place a huge lien on your little home.

- If you have a HUD (Department of Housing and Urban Development) loan, closing the first day of the month as opposed to the last day of the previous month will cost you one entire month's interest. On a conventional loan, the same situation would cost you one day's interest. Interesting.

- Communicate with the institution that holds the loan secured by your property. Talk to your agent.

SELLER'S AGENT

At the execution of the sales contract, the seller's agent should have made the sellers aware of the approximate amount of money they will net from the sale of their home. Since that time, some unexpected expenses could have occurred, such as termite repair, repairs required by the lender, or removal of a lien or other encumbrance. As these problems arise and are resolved, the seller's agent will rework the figures to let the seller know the new net amount of proceeds from the sale.

The seller's agent will work with the buyer's agent, the lender, and the closing attorney to schedule repairs, final inspection (walk-throughs), and, finally, the closing. They will then don the appropriate Ward or June Cleaver face and head to the closing to meet the Haskells.

Hints to Seller's Agent:

- All the work you have done in the past will be quickly forgotten if you have made an error or failed to notify the seller of an expense that appears on the closing statement.

- Get any "surprising" information from the closing attorney, examine it, and be prepared to react quickly, if necessary.

- Say hello to Wally and the Beaver.

The Closing

Chapter 13

Foreclosures

Fool's Gold

Non-real estate people have considered foreclosures to be the best deal in real estate since the day Manhattan was traded away by the Indians for a few beads. This misconception has been perpetuated by some unscrupulous people who have written books and conducted seminars telling people how much money Jane X. Public can make in the purchase and resale of foreclosures. (And I thought buyers and sellers were liars!)

How do you think a foreclosure happens? Could it be that the lender hides in the bushes (pardon me, shrubbery) and waits until the precise moment that the homeowner has the home in its most perfect condition. Then, before the unsuspecting borrower can say "due process," the lender forecloses. The whole process must take about ten minutes.

The best is yet to come. The lending institution then sells the property for approximately one-tenth of what it costs to foreclose because of an obscure tax law that is unknown to anyone except hustlers of "get rich quick" books and a friend of a friend of a friend who knows someone who bought a foreclosure for $3,000 and sold it for a million. For some reason, this someone still works at the same job he has had for the last twelve years and drives a '77 LeSabre with a rotten dashboard.

BUYER

Buyers are misinformed about the value of foreclosures. Lending institutions, although now deregulated so as to be able to be unprofitable in more than one state, are nevertheless still governed as to what price they can sell a property. In foreclosures they usually are particularly regulated, and are therefore unable to accept anything other than appraised value for the first several months.

These foreclosed properties are referred to as OREO (Other Real Estate Owned) or REO (Real Estate Owned). Each lending institution has a department that deals with REOs. The heads of these departments are frequently a whipping post of officers' meetings. The reason for this is that the officers who initially lent the monies for the purchase of the REO properties can't believe that the REO department head can't receive offers better than those that actually came forth.

Many times, in an effort to move these properties, the lender will offer better than market rates with which to finance these undesirable properties. In condominium purchases, this may cause problems — especially if the new owner should need to sell the property. If the development is not approved by Fannie Mae or her cousin Freddie Mac, the new purchaser will not be able to obtain financing. In short, the buyer of the REO may have gotten a great price with unbelievable terms. However, the property may not be sellable.

Hints to Buyer:

- If you're searching for the deal of a lifetime, read the next chapter. This chapter is about foreclosures, and they are not the deal of a lifetime.

- If you must buy a foreclosure, do so with the same caution and discretion that you would use with a non-foreclosure.

- There's a reason that the previous owner allowed the foreclosure. The property wouldn't sell.

BUYER'S AGENT

The buyers had heard of the friend of a friend of a friend who made a million on a foreclosure. For some reason, buyers don't view foreclosed properties as they do non-REO properties. They are excited, and the little things don't matter. They don't want their bubble burst. Visions of gold at the end of their rainbows often cause the sellers to beat a path to the nearest bank and sign anything placed before them.

Hints to Buyer's Agent:

- Treat the REO just as you would any other property. Provide a CMA and explain the value of the property.

- Deal with the lender as you would any other seller.

- Understand the pressure on the lender's representatives who must deal with you. They are accustomed to receiving offers that would make other sellers slit their wrists. And if you think a spouse or Ma or Pa can be tough, try a table full of bankers.

SELLER

The sellers in this chapter are corporations. The particular corporation has spent a rather tidy sum of money on the foreclosure, and now it is a property owner by default. Literally. The previous owner probably tried every way in the world to keep the property out of foreclosure — that is, to sell it — but could not. Now the lender must try to sell it. They order an appraisal. They must list the property for the appraised amount or their basis (which includes acquisition and foreclosure fees), whichever is greater.

The property is almost always empty and often poorly maintained. There are reasons the lender owns it. Neverthless, a naive public views the property as a deal, which often causes stupid offers.

Hints to Seller:

- Reject stupid offers. Let the buyer know you are a lender, not a giver.

- List the property with a licensed, real estate agent. They will ally themselves with you as you face the sharks.

SELLER'S AGENT

The agent for the lender (seller) must deal with (or duck) calls from every variety of quack out there. These callers have seen the television ads, spent a fortune on a book filled with misinformation (lies, if you will), and now they are official, card-carrying entrepreneurs. They need to be reprogrammed and debugged of the hype they have ingested in order that the agent doesn't waste hours with this version of the next Donald Trump.

Hints to Seller's Agent:

- Educate the buyers to the fact that your responsibility to the lender is the same as your responsbility to any seller.

- Don't advertise the property as a foreclosure.

- Tell the fools not to count their gold.

Chapter 14

The Deal of a Lifetime

Yes, Virginia, There Is a Santa Claus

One morning a man called me and told me that he had heard I could get him "the deal of a lifetime." I informed him that I had been fortunate enough to work with people who had fared rather well in their real estate investments. We then spoke about his situation, resources, goals, and other pertinent data. He was very open with me and several times told me that he did not want "just a good deal" or even "a great deal." He wanted "the deal of a lifetime."

I assured him I would keep an ear to the ground and use all my resources in an attempt to get him his deal. Furthermore, I promised that I would not call him until I had found the absolute deal of a lifetime. That afternoon, the man called again. He informed me that he had left his home for about thirty minutes and had forgotten to engage his telephonic answering apparatus, so he had probably missed my call.

"What call?" I asked.

"Well, it has been three hours," he explained. "Haven't you found it yet?"

"Found what?"

"The deal of a lifetime," he screamed.

I had failed him.

When people decide they want the deal of a lifetime, they mean the deal of the lifetime of a housefly (about twenty-four hours).

BUYER

There is a Santa Claus. He has elves. In real estate circles, elves are disguised as real estate agents, lenders, and closing attorneys. The reindeer are the MLS and the network of agents. The deal of a lifetime will raise its head on occasion and may appear as an agent's mistake, a seller's mistake, a corporate buyout, an estate sale, a home lacking street appeal, a secret, or, O.K., once in many lifetimes of deal-finding...a foreclosure.

Christmas can come at any time. If you haven't been a good boy or girl (karma again), you will not receive the gift. Be good and have your jolly elf (agent) on the lookout for the DOL (Deal of a Lifetime). On occasion, an agent from an area that does not demand a high dollar per square foot will venture into uncharted waters without the help of a map (CMA). Or maybe an ogre, in an effort to greedle an agent, will price his house too low.

Multiple-heir estate sales are often profitable. For example, if there are five heirs and if buyers and sellers are $1,000 apart in price, that represents only $200 per heir. These negotiations can become very intense due to the emotional facade. If one heir gets too tense, step outside for some fresh heir.

Some companies will arrange for the purchase of an employee's home if they transfer the employee. A relocation specialty firm will usually handle the sale for the corporation. They purchase the property at a discounted price and attempt to profit from the sale. If the relocation company obtained an unusually low appraisal and negotiated a low buyout, a DOL is in the works.

Hints to Buyer:

- Get to know Santa Claus (an agent) and his elves.
- When the real-estatic Christmas comes, regardless of the month, put out your cookies and milk (earnest money).
- Be nice.

BUYER'S AGENT

Buyer's agents have been warned not to come back to the buyer unless they return with the deal of a lifetime. They must work with the buyer in arranging the financing, the inspection, and the closing prior to finding the property that is soon to become the deal.

Deals do not stay on the market long. If a suspect comes on the market, the agent must act quickly and efficiently. The inspector should attend the first showing. There may not be time for a second showing before the deal is a notch in someone else's six- shooter. The agent realizes the offer must be clean because it will probably be presented with several others. A clean contract for a lower price is worth more than a higher, contingency-loaded offer.

Hints to Buyer's Agent:

- Work with the elves. Have the reindeer bridled and hitched to the sleigh.
- Convince the buyer to submit a cash, no-inspection, quick-closing offer. (This applies only to the deal of a lifetime.)
- Communicate. Some lesser agent will sell them a lesser deal.

SELLER

The seller sold the house too low for some reason. It could make sense, maybe not.

Hint to Seller:

- No one made you sign the contract. You have no one to blame but yourself.

SELLER'S AGENT

The seller's agent understands the needs of the seller. Perhaps a quick, low sale will allow the seller to realize a profit in another area.

Hints to Seller's Agent:

- Don't blow it.
- Don't worry. Everybody loves Santa Claus.

Afterwards

Living Happily Ever After

Now you're ready. Your mission, should you decide to acccept it, lies before you. You can prevail. Assemble your team and press on.

Laugh in the face of ogres. Stand strong in proud defense against the Greedles. Open your heart, soul, and closet to Woodward and Bernstein. Sing with the crickets.

You now know how to achieve your goal. Ally thyself with thy agent and prepare for the excitment. Brew some tea in the kettle as Ma and Pa Meddle. Place a ladder against the wall for the inspector. Leave your love light on for the ETs. This is going to be fun. You'll see.

I hope you'll enjoy your real estate experiences as much as I have, and that the little ditties in this book have proved helpful. Tell all your friends.

Spread the Word

If you would like to order additional copies of *Buyers Are Liars and Sellers Are Too,* you may do so either by completing and mailing in this form with payment, or by calling the phone number listed below.

Please send me ___ copies of *Buyers Are Liars and Sellers Are Too* at $6.95 per copy for a total order amount of $_____.

Tennessee residents only: Add 8.25% ($0.57 per book) state sales tax.

Total amount enclosed $_____.

SHIP TO:

Name_____

Address_____

City_____State_____ZIP_____

Return this form with check or money order payable to:

Eggman Publishing
2908 Poston Avenue
Suite 201
Nashville, TN 37203

Or order by phone with Visa or MasterCard by calling (615) 327-9390, weekdays between 9 a.m. and 5 p.m. Central Time.